W9-ADN-604

TIDE
POOLS

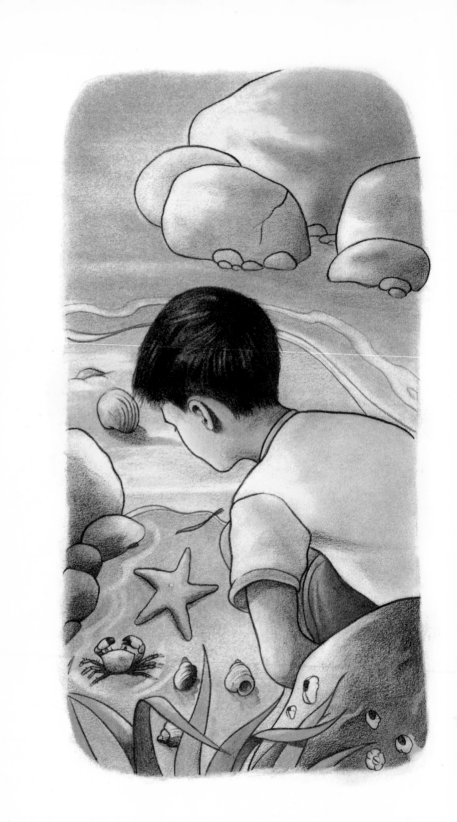

A HARPERCOLLINS NATURE STUDY BOOK

TIDE POOLS

by Ronald Rood
illustrated by Martin Classen

HarperCollins*Publishers*

J 574.92
ROOD

And God created great whales, and every wild creature
that moveth, which the waters brought forth abundantly,
after their kind . . . and God saw that it was good.
—*Genesis 1:21*

The illustrations in this book were done in colored pencil with charcoal
on Cold Pressed illustration board.

Text copyright © 1993 by Ronald Rood
Illustrations copyright © 1993 by Martin Classen
All rights reserved. Printed in the United States of America. For information address
HarperCollins Children's Books, a division of HarperCollins Publishers,
10 East 53rd Street, New York, NY 10022.
Designed by Harriett Barton

Library of Congress Cataloging-in-Publication Data
Rood, Ronald N.
  Tide pools / by Ronald Rood ; illustrated by Martin Classen.
      p.   cm.
  "A HarperCollins Nature Study Book."
  Includes bibliographical references.
  Summary: Introduces the many kinds of sea creatures that can be found in tide pools, including
starfish, molluscs, crustaceans, and jellyfish.
    ISBN 0-06-027074-8. — ISBN 0-06-027075-6 (lib. bdg.)
    1. Marine biology—Juvenile literature.   2. Tide pools—Juvenile literature.   [1. Marine animals.
2. Tide pools.]   I. Classen, Martin, ill.   II. Title.   III. Series.
QH91.16.R64   1993   92-2581
574.92—dc20   CIP
                                                                                         AC

1   2   3   4   5   6   7   8   9   10
❖
First Edition

To our four flourishin' young 'uns:
Jan, Tom, Ali, and Rog—
with whom your mother and I have enjoyed
many happy hours between the tides—
this book is dedicated with much love
—*Dad*

For my mother
who always encouraged the artist in my dreams
—*M.C.*

Contents

At the Seashore

The ocean waves splash and crash along the shore. The foaming water rushes up the beach, pauses, and goes back again. It chuckles and gurgles among the rocks and fills little depressions in the sand.

Jellyfish, shrimp, fish and their eggs, water fleas, and many other creatures are carried by these waves. Driftwood and floating seaweeds act as rafts whose passengers may include snails and crabs.

The water keeps advancing until the tide is full. Then the sea begins to retreat. It drains away from the beach, leaving tide pools in rocky cavities and sandy hollows. The floating water life joins the crawlers and creepers and swimmers who were already there.

No two tide pools are ever the same. One may hold fifty snails and half a dozen kinds of fish. Another may be a home for a crusty old crab, three starfish, and a dozen shrimp. Sculpins—little fish with big, froglike mouths—often live in west coast rock pools. Each pool is a marine aquarium, full of secrets and surprises as it awaits the return of the sea.

Scratchy and Spiny

Can you lie on your stomach and creep along without moving your arms or legs? You could, if you were a starfish.

How does the starfish do it? Pick one up and you'll find the answer. On its underside are hundreds of little moving structures that look like tiny fingers. The starfish pumps water into these "tube feet," as they are called, so they expand or contract like balloons. Pushing and pulling, the busy little tube feet move this surprising creature over the sand and rocks.

Tube feet can also act as suction cups. To open a clam, the starfish wraps itself around the clam's two shells. Slowly and steadily those tube feet pull the shells apart. Then the starfish can eat the clam.

An adult starfish glides slowly along, but when it was young it moved more quickly. Newly hatched starfish are active little babies, using tiny hairs, or cilia, to swim through the water. Then, as they grow, they settle down to their slow life on the bottom of the ocean.

If you handle a starfish too roughly, one of its arms might break off. People who are angry with the starfish because it eats clams and oysters may break it in pieces, too. This really doesn't help, however. The larger pieces just grow into new starfish. Then, instead of just one, there are several of them!

Most starfish feel scratchy and almost prickly to the touch. Their relatives have this rough skin, too, and may also be found in tide pools. The most prickly is the sea urchin, whose spines make it look like a handful of

thorns. Smaller spines, more like hairs, are found on the sand dollar. They make it look like a fuzzy cookie, there on the sandy bottom.

Sea cucumbers may be found in tide pools, too. The spines are buried in their warty skin. They look something like the garden vegetable.

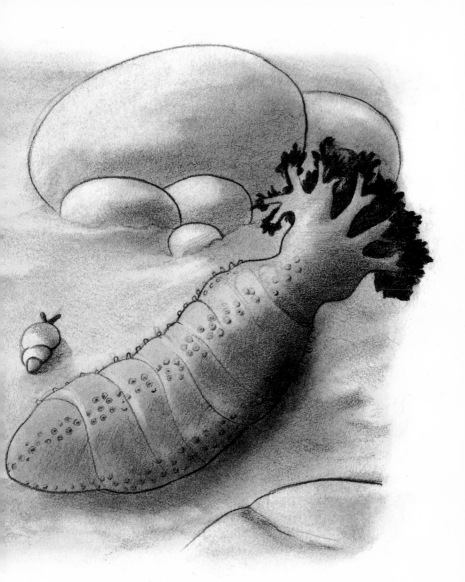

The sea cucumber spreads leafy-looking tentacles out into the water. When small sea creatures have been caught on those sticky arms, the cucumber puts each tentacle into its mouth and pulls the unfortunate victims off— just as you'd lick jelly off your fingers!

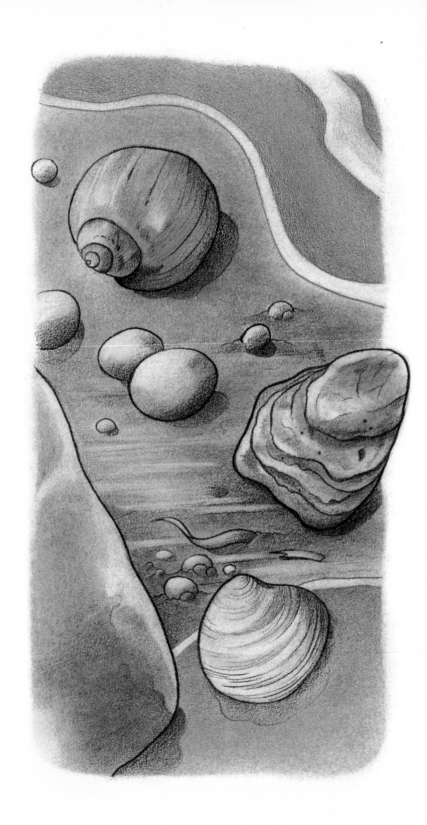

Soft Bodies, Hard Shells

Suppose you had no bones in your body and were as soft as a marshmallow. There in your tide pool you might find yourself surrounded by hungry fish and sharp-eyed birds. How can you keep out of trouble?

This is the problem facing the creatures known as molluscs. Soft and squishy as they are, most of them protect themselves by building sturdy shells. You may find them—clams, oysters, limpets, chitons, and snails—in almost any tide pool.

One of the most common snails is the periwinkle. These little creatures look like gray marbles. They creep along, scraping tiny plants known as algae from the surfaces of underwater objects. When the tide goes down, the periwinkles cling tightly to the rock, keeping moist in their shells until the waves return again.

Each of the many kinds of snail has its own kind of shell. You may find small red shells, large white ones, round ones, pointed ones— each made by a soft-bodied mollusc and used for a home all its life. As the snail grows, it adds to the shell, so it is always protected by a house that fits the shape of its body.

mussels

Periwinkles and most other snails make shells that curl into spirals. Limpets live on rocks under shells like tiny upside-down saucers. Chitons have oval bodies protected by jointed shells.

Clams and oysters have two shells. The shells may open to take in water and floating particles of food, or they may close for protection. Mussels, with their blue-black shells, attach themselves to rocks or driftwood or even to each other. You can often see them by the thousands in a tide pool.

One of the prettiest of shells is made by the scallop. Sometimes called "sea butterfly," the scallop opens and closes its shells, dancing through the water like a butterfly. The scallop you eat is actually the muscle that operates these delicate shells.

The most active molluscs of all are the

squid

slender squid and the graceful octopus. Normally found in deeper water, they may wash into a tide pool in a storm. These creatures have no outer shells and can creep by means of their tentacles. If an enemy threatens them, they may squirt water out through a tube, shooting themselves backward out of danger. So, long before airplanes and jet skis, they were travelling by jet propulsion!

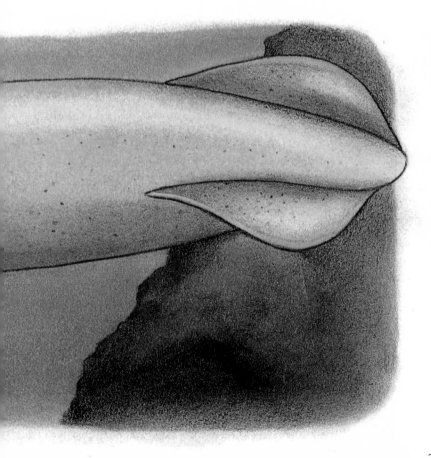

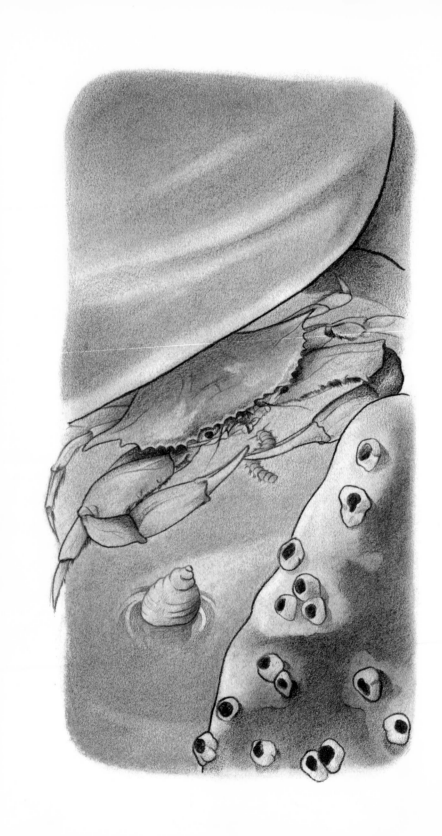

The Crusty Ones

There are few creatures more crabby than a crab. It seems forever ready for a fight. So be careful—a crab will nip you if it gets a chance.

There's a good reason the crab is so feisty. Fish, gulls, eels—and even an octopus—will eat it if they can. So it's always on the defensive.

Tide pools can be homes for several kinds of crabs. Rock crabs of many kinds and colors hide under stones or prowl along the bottom. Some kinds even wander on rocks out of the water. They will eat almost anything, from a bit of seaweed to some unlucky worm. Swimming eastern blue crabs and speckled lady crabs may even catch small fish.

If we lose an arm or leg it is gone forever. A crab will replace a lost leg or claw when it molts, or sheds its crusty outer skin. The new leg begins as a little bud when the crab molts. The bud gets larger with the next molt, and so on until a new leg is formed. Many of the crab's cousins, including lobsters, can also re-place lost parts in this way after an argument or an escape from an enemy.

Many tide pools are homes for little swim-ming "water fleas." These are not really fleas, but relatives of the crab, and they look like

grains of rice that have suddenly grown legs. When they leave the water and hide under dried seaweed, they are called "beach fleas." Pick up the dry seaweed and they'll hop around as fast as real fleas—jumping everywhere like popcorn.

Inch-long shrimp, looking like tiny lobsters, crawl and swim through the water. One kind, the glass shrimp, is so transparent you can see its beating heart. Like beach fleas and all the crab family, they grow by shedding their skins.

Barnacles are also members of the crab family. They attach to almost any object, from driftwood to an old tin can. They are even found on sea turtles and whales. Each barnacle has protective scales or plates that open or close around its body much as you can close your cupped hands. To feed, the barnacle sticks its feathery legs out between these shells and scoops food into its mouth.

The hermit crab lives with its tender hind end tucked into an old snail shell. Then, with

its strong legs and claws, it wanders over the sandy bottom, protected by the shell as it looks for food or a fight.

The horseshoe crab, shaped like an upside-down soup plate with a spiky tail, is not a crab at all. It is really a harmless relative of the spider. Now it is found only on the Atlantic coast, but its ancestors roamed the world's seas long before the age of the dinosaurs. So when you find a horseshoe crab, you are really in the presence of a walking, swimming, living fossil.

Jelly in the Ocean

If you should happen to see a glassy circle the size of a saucer on the sand, look again. It may be the remains of a jellyfish. Made almost entirely of water, this transparent creature may dry up to almost nothing when it's washed up on the sand.

A jellyfish in a tide pool is more lucky. Shaped like an umbrella, it swims by opening and closing every few seconds. Hanging beneath its edge are several arms, or tentacles, that bear stinging cells. When a small fish or other creature brushes against these arms, it may be stung so it cannot swim away. Then the tentacles move the victim to the jellyfish's mouth. Large swimmers like humans may be stung, too, but seldom seriously hurt.

Jellyfish come in many colors and sizes. Small ones may be no bigger than this letter "O." The largest can be six feet across. Try to fit that one into your tide pool!

One cousin of the jellyfish that can be found in tide pools is the sea anemone. It looks like an undersea flower, but its petals are really stinging tentacles. To see how the

tentacles act, drop a bit of fish or meat on the anemone. The tentacles close around the food and take it to the waiting mouth.

Small relatives of the anemone build limy tubes around their bodies. The creatures in these tubes, known as polyps, produce more inhabitants like themselves. Tube building continues until a large mass, known as coral, is

produced. Most corals live in warm waters, but you may find a few as far north as Cape Cod on the Atlantic coast, and California in the west. Look at a living coral with a magnifying glass and you'll see tiny tentacles stretched out and waiting for their dinners to swim by.

The Great Barrier Reef, near Australia, is

more than a thousand miles long. It is largely made up of coral, as are tropical atolls and reefs in the Bahamas east of Florida. The tip of Florida, too, rests on an ancient coral reef, as do some islands in the Caribbean—resting on limy structures built long ago by those tiny bits of living jelly in the sea.

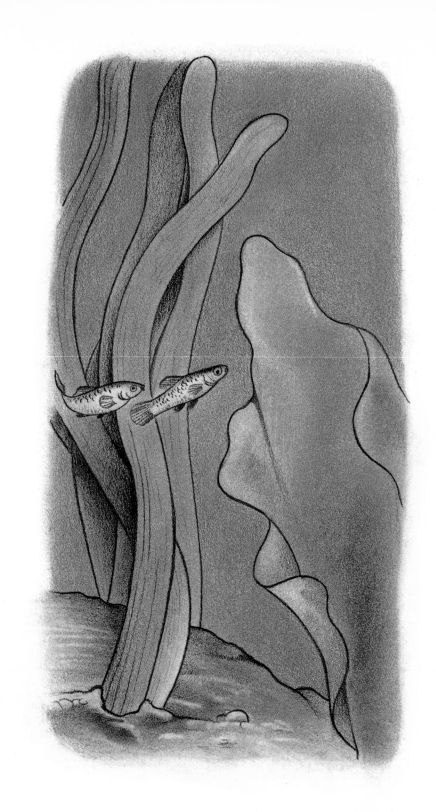

Undersea Forest

Did you know there might have been seaweed in the ice cream you had for dessert? Or that seaweed could have helped give a silky, shiny finish to your shirt or slacks?

These are just two of the ways people use the smooth substance known as alginate found in many seaweeds. This material also helps give seaweeds their slippery appearance.

Although called weeds, these plants are not really weeds at all. A weed is usually thought of as having little value, but seaweeds are important to the lives of ocean creatures—and not only as food. Snails and sea worms lay their eggs on them. Fish, crabs, shrimp, and sea horses live among their stems and fronds.

You may find these plants, also known as

algae, washed into tide pools after a storm. They may be in colors of red, green, or brown. Two of the best-known types are kelp and rockweed. Kelp is long, flat, and tough, like a leather strap. It attaches to rocks and shells—often to a clam or mussel. Then, in a storm, the whole thing washes up on shore

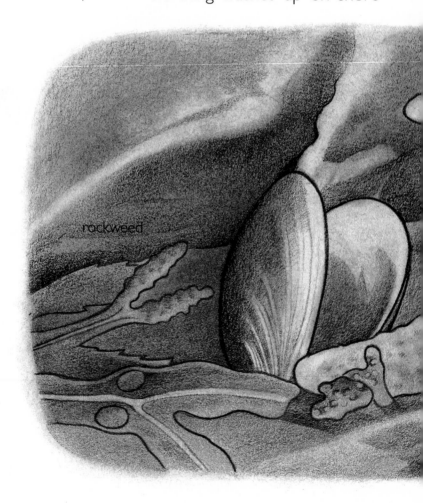

rockweed

and into tide pools—kelp, clam, and all.

Rockweeds are flat and branching with little air bladders on the leaves to help float them as the water rises. They often grow so close together they may cover a tide pool completely. Lift them up, however, and you'll find a world of water creatures hidden from

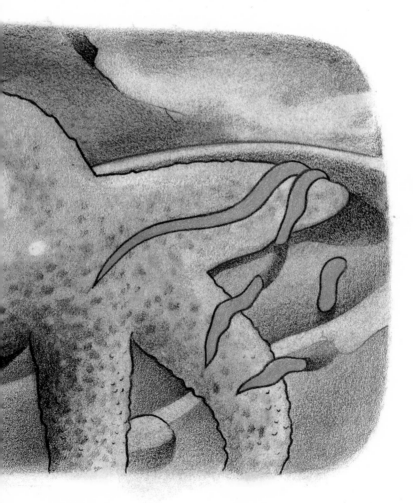

sea lettuce

gulls and other birds by the rockweed.

A common red seaweed is known as Irish moss. It is short and branching, like a little tree four inches tall. People dry Irish moss and use it as food, but it takes a long time to chew.

Among the green seaweeds the brightest in color is sea lettuce. Thin and crinkly like a lettuce leaf, this plant is often collected by people for food. Periwinkles may eat it too, as do some kinds of crabs and ducks.

You'll find other kinds of seaweeds in almost any tide pool. Codium, or green fleece, is dark greenish-black and looks like a many-fingered glove. The east coast sea colander is a brown kelp that looks as if it has been shot full of holes. Mermaid's hair resembles tangled wiry grass that should have been mowed.

sea colander

Eelgrass, with its long, bright-green blades, sometimes drifts into the tide pool from shallows along the shore. It is not a seaweed, but more closely related to pond lilies and other freshwater plants. Baby scallops cling to eelgrass, while many kinds of fish and snails and sea worms find homes among its leaves. Eelgrass is a favorite of a sea-shore goose known

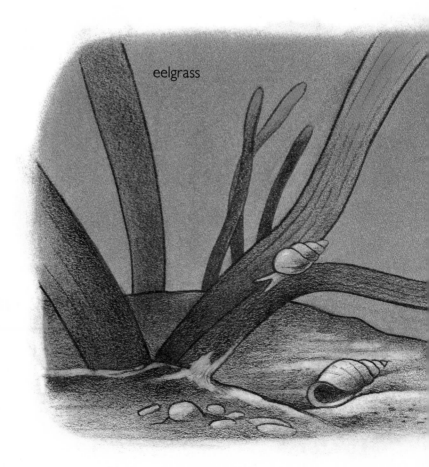

eelgrass

as brant. So, for food and shelter, it is one of the most important plants of the seashore.

There they are in their watery seaweed forest—starfish and snails, crabs and jellyfish, and water plants. They pass their entire lives unseen and unknown—unless we squat down to have a look. Then, for a little while, we too can join the fascinating world of the tide pool.

Your Visit to
a Tide Pool

When you approach a tide pool, be careful of your shadow. Do not let it fall across the pool, as it may frighten the residents. Then, after you have arrived, be perfectly still for several minutes. You'll see things beginning to move that may have appeared lifeless at first.

If you want to examine something closely, place it gently in a light-colored dish of seawater. Put only a few creatures in any container at a time, as they will quickly use up the oxygen in the water. Unless you are going to put the captives back quickly, keep the dish out of the sun so it will remain as cool as possible.

Clues to Naming Tide-Pool Creatures

starfish showing tube feet

If you see a tide-pool creature with rubbery, stretchy tube feet, you'll know it's a member of the starfish family. These tube feet stretch in lines away from the center like those on the arms of a starfish. Even the sea cucumber has tube feet, which extend backward along its body.

clam   sea snail

No legs, a tender body, and a hard shell—these are the marks of the tide-pool molluscs. Clams, oysters, and mussels have two shells that open and shut like hinged doors. A snail has a curled shell that perfectly fits its body.

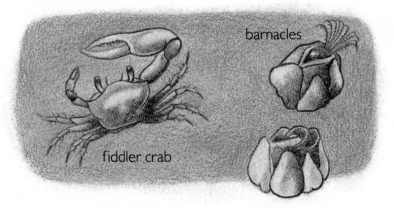

barnacles

fiddler crab

Legs like jointed sticks and a crusty skin covering the body are the trademarks of the crab family. Some, like the beach fleas, are active swimmers and jumpers. Others live in one place, like the barnacles in their limy little forts on tidal rocks.

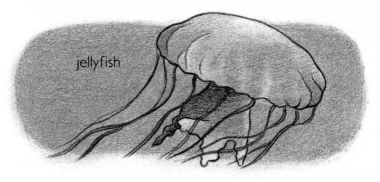

jellyfish

The jellyfish family is well named. Its members look like a blob of jelly when out of the water. In the sea, however, they become delicate circles or tubes with graceful arms or tentacles around the edge.

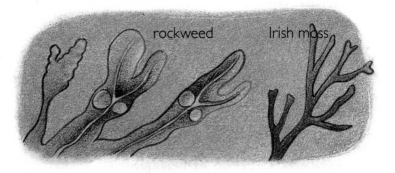

rockweed   Irish moss

Colorful seaweeds provide food and shelter for tide-pool creatures. They serve as nests and nurseries for many kinds of fishes. Some seaweeds stretch a hundred feet and more from bottom to surface of deeper waters. When storms tear them loose, they drift to shore. Catching on rocks and washing into hollows, these wanderers become part of the tangled seaweed forests of the tide pools.

Would You Like to Know More?

There is more to a tide pool than any single book can tell you. You may find sponges in a pool, for instance, and worms that can stretch as far as your arms can reach; jellyfish that shine in the dark; dozens of kinds of fish, some that can change their color; and worms that swim and fish that crawl. All live in this seashore world.

Here are a few books that tell more of the interesting world of the beach. Books especially good for young readers are marked with an asterisk (*).

*Abbott, R. Tucker. *Golden Nature Guide to Seashores*. New York: Golden Press, Inc., 1962.

*Arnold, Augusta F. *The Sea-Beach at Ebb-Tide*. New York: Dover Publications, Inc., 1968.

*Buck, Margaret Waring. *Along the Seashore*. Nashville, TN: Abingdon Press, 1964.

Gosner, Kenneth L. *A Field Guide to the Atlantic Seashore*. Peterson Field Guide Series. Boston: Houghton Mifflin Company, 1982.

Kaplan, Eugene. *A Field Guide to Coral Reefs of the Caribbean and Florida*. Peterson Field Guide Series. Boston: Houghton Mifflin Company, 1991.

*McConnaughey, Bayard, and Evelyn Mc-Connaughey. *Pacific Coast*. Ed. by Charles Elliott. Audubon Society Nature Guide Series. New York: Alfred A. Knopf, Inc., 1985.

Morris, Percy. *A Field Guide to Pacific Coast Shells*. Peterson Field Guide Series. Boston: Houghton Mifflin Company, 1974.

*Rood, Ronald. *Beachcombers All*. Shelburne, VT: New England Press, 1990.